Mind Your MIND!
#ThinkAboutIt
Mastering Your State of Mind
7 Mindset Principles

By: Dr. Sharron Credle

Copyright

Cover Design: Mr. Van Johnson <u>vexedgraphics@yahoo.com</u>

Acknowledgements

Giving God the glory for all He has done. I thank God for using me as the vessel to publish this work. I am truly honored to be on this journey to help others shift their mindset so that they can experience all God has for them on this side of Heaven.

I also thank my circle of family and friends for your continued support and encouragement during the writing of this project. God intentionally placed each of you in my life to help me be the best me. Without a doubt, I know that I am truly blessed to have you in my life. You know who you are!

Dedication

I humbly dedicate this book to everyone struggling with mastering their mindset. Please know that you are not alone. The 7 mindset principles were created with you in mind. You don't need permission to change your mindset. It is the best gift you can give yourself so that you can live your best authentic life.

Table of Contents

Introduction

Every human being has a state of mind that influences their thinking, behavior and attitude. The state of mind is the driving force for all that we do. Whether it is a healthy mind, a traumatized mind or a chemically imbalanced mind, our actions are an authentic reflection of our state of mind.

Per an online dictionary (Bing), the mind is defined as "the element of a person that enables them to be aware of the world and their experiences, to think, and to feel; the faculty of consciousness and thought." We cannot always control what thoughts enter our MIND, but we can control them by how we choose to act or not act upon them.

Although the brain is made up of many specialized areas that work together, thinking and voluntary movements begin in the cortex which is the outer layer of the brain (webmd). The brain is also made up of many lobes and the frontal lobes are responsible for problem solving, judgment and motor function. As a side note, the frontal lobe fully develops around the age of 25 in typically developing brains. That is why you often hear parents say "it seems like the light bulb came on" because they see the connections being made in their young adult child's thinking and actions. They begin to align.

So why is this important? Why write a book about this topic? Simple! It's fascinating! I have always been intrigued with human behavior...my own in particular. My intrigue and passion intensified after becoming a professional Special Educator, Counselor and Leader of others. While also taking the time to reflect on some of my own actions as well as observing the actions of others. Over the years and during multiple conversations with strangers, friends, family, students, mentees and coaching clients, I realized that our problem-solving skills and judgement impacts us in ways that we are not always aware of. I also concluded that my perspective on topics of behavior was often times different and unique than others. Sometimes as awkward as it was to share my voice, I did it anyway because I had learned to accept that was how the Holy Spirit used me in those moments and that my input was needed, valued and used to change an action or conversation.

It is important to note here that just because something is difficult does not mean it should be avoided.

How did I get to this realization? I began asking myself and others... Why did I/you do that? What was I (were you) thinking? What would make me/you do such a thing? Why am I/you having those thoughts? Upon deep reflection, I came to the conclusion that those actions were triggered by a thought. Yes, a thought! A thought so powerful that you follow through with the action either positive or negative.

Mind Your MIND: #ThinkAboutIt – Mastering Your State of Mind (7 Mindset Principles) is a self-help book that discusses my perspective on the topic and how I learned to Mind my State of MIND. My hope is that you will consider it as you explore your thinking process. In other words, it is my prayer that you use it to develop your own mindset bio. Be patient with yourself because it takes roughly 10,000 hours to master anything. This process is not going to be business as usual. You are going to enter into the mindset of being the boss of your mind and no longer operate in a drunken state of mind.

With full disclosure, I am not a medical doctor nor do I have any experience as a licensed therapist, phycologist, or physiatrist. However, I have life experiences and am often sought out to provide my perspective on personal and professional situations related to this topic. I now understand that I have been called to do this work because God has given me a gift and the courage to ask questions that forces people to look below the iceberg to a deeper level of conversation. Many people approach conversations by dealing with the behavior and not the thinking behind the behavior. The latter is critical to helping people transform their thinking and actions. Mastering your state of mind is everything! It's transformative!

This book is structured to allow you the opportunity to reflect on each chapter's topic by addressing the #ThinkAboutIt question(s) at the end of the chapter with additional notes pages in the appendix. For extended work, this book can also be used in conjunction with my self-published writing journal "The Dr. S.D.C. Structured Journal" Shift the Mindset & The View Will Change (Amazon.com). The journal challenges writers to shift their mindset so that the view of their circumstances will change and therefore, influence appropriate actions.

So, as you read this book, approach it with the goal of learning something new or confirming some things you already knew and maybe use it to help someone else. At the end of each section, you will be able to share your thoughts in written form about the topic.

The Big Reveal!

I distinctly remember the moment when it became apparent to me that God designed me to share His voice boldly when directed to do so. Although, the awareness was always there, the maturity, acceptance, and understanding was not. In the Spring of 2007, I entered a hospital in New York with my husband and a few other family members to visit his best childhood girlfriend. For some reason, everyone entered the room before me to greet the patient. As I crossed the threshold, I vividly recall a strong feeling or force literally take over my being. I sat in a chair quietly observing the dynamics going on in that hospital room as an outsider looking into a closed group. Of course at the time, I could not explain what I was feeling and no one else knew what I was experiencing.

As the conversation ensued about her condition, she revealed that many years prior the doctor found a lump in her breast and recommended treatment. However, because of her strong faith in God, she decided to allow Him to heal her. What she said next is what got my undivided attention. She went on to state that although she and her mother were extremely close, she had not told her mother about her diagnosis of breast cancer. Her husband and young child were not completely aware of the extent of her condition either. After that confession, no one in the room said anything to question her about why she had not shared her condition with mother.

As the visit was coming to its end, the family gathered to pray with her and say our goodbyes. But that strong force commanded me to say what I was given, even though I did not know the lady very well. So I obediently said to her that I thought she should tell her mother what was going on since they experienced a close relationship because her mother would be heart broken to know she was sick and she did not tell her if her condition got worse. It would have probably left her mother searching for an answer for the rest of her life. After I finished, I felt like I was floating along. We left and went to our next destination and I still had not shared my experience with anyone. But the conversation in the car was that they were glad I shared with her.

Upon returning home the next day, I received a phone call from my husband's friend thanking me for what I told her. As a result, she called her mother and shared her diagnosis. Instantly her mother was in route to New York to be with her. A few days after her mother's arrival, God called her home. From that experience forward, I learned to listen to my inner voice and to focus on the thoughts being placed in my mind to be shared through words and actions.

My Mindset Bio:

I am clear that I was created by God through man to execute His purpose for me on earth. I see the glass half full not half empty. I have a positive mindset no matter what and believe it is critical for your overall health mentally, physically, and spiritually. I believe I can have it all—that is—all that God has predestined for me. I am confident and strong. I understand that people come into our lives for a season and for a reason which allows me to make those adjustments very easily without taking it personally. I am not easily offended. I am happy and celebrate others when they succeed. I am unique. God did not create anyone else like me. The Holy Spirit resides within me. I am not in competition with anyone else. I love me. I am a continuous work in progress. I carry the responsibility of eliminating some of my family's generational conditions.

My faith and belief in God is unwavering. I'm not perfect so I don't put that kind of pressure on myself. I care for my mind health by what I take in. I protect my mind space by the types of conversations I engage in. I am not a gossiper. I am comfortable with saying no and I am comfortable with saying yes. I don't put people on a pedestal. I am realistic and optimistic. I am led by the Holy Spirit. I am courageous. I am bold. I am determined. I am the author of my own story. I am not a quitter. I am intelligent. I am confident. I am strong. I am nonjudgmental. I am a gray area thinker most of the time. I am an encourager. I believe in reconciliation and work towards it with broken or bruised relationships. I don't sweat the small things. I am generally cool, calm, and collected under pressure. I ask questions to gather additional information for understanding. I am an ambivert, I have the balance of extrovert and introvert features. I strive to correct my imperfections daily. I am a mentor and a coach. I am complicated at times depending on the significance of the matter. I am so much more. I am enough!

Your Mindset Bio

Write Your Bio: The purpose of writing your bio is to establish your mindset prior to reading the book. As you read, reflect on some of the thoughts presented as it relates to how you Mind Your State of MIND.

Name:

_____

What's your general state of mind?

_____

_____

_____

(extra notes pages at the back of the book)

How do you care for your mind health?

_____

_____

_____

_____

_____

_____

_____

_____

_____

_____

_____

_____

_____

_____

_____

_____

_____

_____

(extra notes pages at the back of the book)

Principle 1: Shift Your Mindset & Your View Will Change

"Mind Your State of MIND"

Life is full of experiences that call us to action. Some of those experiences are out of our control while others are orchestrated by our thinking and therefore our decisions. The key to navigating any experience is connected to our state of mind. You've seen people who have forgiven someone they did not know who committed an unimaginable act of violence against them or a loved one. You have also seen people who have lost jobs and walked away without any concerns about what was next. Perhaps it was you. Did you stop to ask yourself why you offer forgiveness to that person? Because surely that person doesn't deserve forgiveness. *He or she really hurt me or violated my trust!* Well some may say that we are commanded to do so by God. Which is true because it is a heart thing. However, every time you think about what that person did to you, your thoughts start to run wild. When the heart and our thinking doesn't align, it is difficult to shift to a different perspective or view of the situation.

Shifting Your Mindset so that *Your View Will Change* requires taking your thoughts captive. Don't allow fleeting thoughts to flee. Catch that thought and try to gain understanding of why you had it – the purpose of it. Some of those fleeting thoughts will take awhile for you to determine their purpose, so write it down and come back to it later. We have more self-developed thoughts than fleeting thoughts. This is where the real work begins.

Self-developed thoughts are a part of our daily functioning (re: family, friends, finances, children, work, etc.). However, what I am going to focus on in this chapter is self-developed thoughts about yourself. Ephesians 4:23 states "to be made new in the attitude of your mind." It doesn't say someone else's mind, it says your own mind.

We spend a lot of time and energy trying to figure out other people's states of mind but not equally or more time thinking about our own state of mind. Your State of Mind is everything! I respectfully assert that it is the most important aspect of who you are and how you approach the world. There is a plethora of widely available data on nutrition, financial health, physical health and dental health along with every other conceivable type of health and we are inundated 24/7 about their importance. Heck, many of us have even purchased the programs from infomercials, social media, and books. But, we are not inundated with literature about the impact our thinking has on our overall success in navigating the many decisions we have to make, although there is a vast amount of information for us to access. Since it takes 10,000 hours to master anything, if you spend that time minding your mind, just imagine what can be accomplished. That is a little more than one year in hours. That commitment must be intentional.

Our will to transform our thinking requires that we research content related to it for those strategies needed to develop our thought processing. For example, think about the ignition and gear shift in a vehicle. There are many details that must all work in synergy to ensure that the vehicle moves when commanded. Your mind works in much the same manner.

Ignition: A vehicle sits in the parked position until a key is inserted or remotely activated to start it. Without that first step, nothing ignites. A thought enters your mind to get it flowing. It awakens the region of the brain which is connected to your feelings, thinking, problem solving, judgment and motor function.

We are constantly shifting our mindset between the on and off position just as we do when we turn the car on and off. The key is to identify where you operate. Is it mainly in the off position or the on position? Are you constantly being ignited by a barrage of thoughts yet they sit in a parked position? Do you find yourself trying to do the right thing then a thought enters your mind which reverses or causes you to change your course of action? Oh yeah and … those dormant thoughts from childhood … those recurring dreams … those are there too.

Reverse: Some of those thoughts can cause you to do a complete change of direction or action contrary to what you were supposed to do. If your thinking is off course, then reverse your thinking and do what you need to do to get back on course. Much like a navigation system, you know you are not thinking straight because your mind keeps playing the same loop over and over. You know when your thinking is on the right track because the thoughts just flow. In other words, you maintain a certain rhythm both personally and professionally.

Neutral: Some thoughts creep in and just lay dormant until another thought enters and triggers action. Those thoughts can live there for many years such as a business idea, a book title, etc. Nothing happens in this state. You spin your wheels rather than moving in any direction. This is not to say that there are not times when you need to pause. Just take care to guard against non-action becoming your normal state.

Drive: Our thoughts push, propel, or press us onward. This is where the action is. It is up to each of us to determine which thoughts to push out and which to propel forward. Just like a car requires you to turn on the ignition, shift the car into drive and press the accelerator to make the car move, the same is true with your thinking. To drive cause and effect, you must turn your brain on with new information, shift to new thinking and apply it to both your words and actions.

To determine where your mindset typically is, it is critical to conduct a self-examination. You can do this by speaking your truth, understanding why it is true then deciding with determination and capacity to do something with your thinking. You accomplish this by investing in your mental health through a process called R.E.F.U.S.E., by no longer being willing to accept faulty thinking and rejecting the notion that this is just how it is.

You know when a child is 2 years old, they begin to understand the power in saying the word "no." They begin to struggle with interdependence and independence. It's a constant battle. Some peoples' thoughts are in a constant state of conflict between positive and negative thinking. This often leads to frustration and inappropriate behavior, failed relationships, self-pity, and other health related concerns such as depression. To transition from conflict to assuredness, you must be bold in what you believe. In other words, R.E.F.U.S.E.

Replay positive thoughts you know about yourself. You are a child of God so that makes you great! Say, you are not perfect and don't pretend that you are. No human being has it all together. Stop replaying negative thoughts in your mind or hurtful things people have said about you. The negativity can cause you to do and say things that don't bring life to your situation. Brain research shows that the brain has a pleasure center (reward center) that lets us know when something is enjoyable and reinforces the desire for us to perform the same pleasurable action again. When you think positively, you activate the pleasure center and are rewarded with regulated emotions, controlled muscle functions, decreased pain, and increased feelings of trust. Now, isn't that what you would like to feel instead of tension?!?! I know that most of us would like more of all of those feelings in our daily life. (health.howstuffworks.com)

Expand your thinking by expanding your experiences. You must intentionally surround yourself with other positive people who engage in conversations that are uplifting and encouraging. In order to know who these people are, practice active listening and become observant. Get out of your own way and let God guide your discernment. This may be strange at first because it may not be your norm. Evoke the Holy Spirit within and you will never be steered wrong. As you expand your thinking and experiences, your state of mind will definitely transform. This transformation will require you to expel people from your circle or redefine your relationships and that's okay.

Forgive yourself first, and forgive others next. Remember, God is a forgiving God so who are you not to forgive yourself for your past? Forgiving others will also release you from having to constantly think about what others said about you or even how they treated you.

Use tools. As you replay positive thoughts, expand your thinking and forgive yourself and others, recognize that we all need help at many junctures in our life. Consider a tool as something used in performing an operation or necessary in the practice of a vocation or profession. The use of tools helps to get us focused. They are go-to resources designed to assist with decision making, shifting our mindset and thinking about life intentionally. What's your favorite scripture(s)? What positive affirmations, do you read and/or recite on a daily basis? What kind of self-talk do you engage in with yourself? Who is in your circle that you can bounce ideas off? Who is in your circle that you admire? Who is your mentor? Who is your coach? Do you exercise consistently? Do you sit in silence, pray or mediate?

Settle it. Stop replaying mistakes in your mind, if you are not going to do anything about it. Stop holding yourself hostage mentally and emotionally. This only happens when you are sick and tired of being sick and tired. You know you are tired when you ask yourself, 'How is this working for me?" What has God said about you? What do you believe about yourself? Stop allowing people to tell you something different about yourself that is not true to make themselves feel or look better than you. Even if the comments are constructive, take what you need to make correction and don't hold on to the other mess. Pay attention to intent. Was the comment said with love and care or was it said to make you feel like the worst person on earth? You will know the difference if you are listening with the Holy Spirit. Settle it also by the types of conversations you find yourself engaging in. If your conversation is not uplifting or providing good advice, then don't engage. Sometimes you have to be bold enough to tell people that you will not entertain a specific conversation and then don't do it.

<u>E</u>xhibit behaviors that demonstrate who you say you are. This right here is it! Who are you? Not who others say you are. Who you are, comes from who God has told you you are. #Thinkaboutit, we were created by the Great I Am which makes each of us an heir of God. You have been justified and redeemed, no matter what you have done. Now, that's powerful. So, why do we not always feel so powerful?

Well, it boils down to your mindset and what you allow to infiltrate your mind. You must get in the posture of not believing everything people say or think about you. Your behaviors must line up with your actions. You cannot be wishy washy or double minded. When your name is called in a circle, is the message consistent? If not, make the correction by shifting your thinking and aligning your actions to your new thinking.

#ThinkAboutIt:

Which letter and description of R.E.F.U.S.E. do you need to develop?

_____

_____

_____

_____

_____

_____

_____

_____

_____

_____

_____

_____

_____

_____

_____

_____

(extra notes pages at the back of the book)

Principle 2:

Mind Your MIND!
Generational Thinking Challenges

#ThinkAboutIt. Mastering your mindset is not an easy feat. As stated in Principle 1, our state of mind influences thinking, behavior, and attitudes. How are our mindsets initially established? More likely than not it's rooted and molded by family thinking patterns. In other words, the majority of our thinking is learned from the adults who are responsible for raising us. They teach us through their words and actions. Did you grow up in a household where your parents said "do as I say not as I do"? That's a confusing message for children who are observing all of our actions. Many of which they will imitate well into adulthood but are clueless as to why. Many of us grew up believing that was how the world operated, saying one thing and doing something else. For some of us, this mindset shifted only when it was not working for us professionally and personally. For so many others, this continues to be their modus operandi.

Why coin this chapter as Generational Challenges vs. Generational Curses? This is a good example of how you Mind Your MIND.

The word curse means "a solemn utterance intended to invoke a supernatural power to inflict harm or punishment on someone or something" (dictionary.com). See I don't believe that there is a supernatural power more powerful than God. I refuse to settle into a mindset that is contrary. We have the power to control how we act out our thoughts. Just because mama, daddy, and your grandfather did it doesn't mean that you have to follow suit particularly if it is damaging. Patterns of behavior and faulty thinking can be disrupted. Ephesians 3:20 says that *"He who is able to do exceedingly abundantly above all that we ask or think, according to the power that worketh in us,"* is how I guide my thinking. Since God can do exceedingly and abundantly above anything that we can think, we may as well think as big as we can and let Him do the rest.

However, what I do understand is that if family members do not share their experiences and patterns of behavior then it continues to get passed down from one generation to the next. Oh the secrets! The secrets can have devastating consequences. For example, on one particular episode of the television show of "Being Mary Jane" her parents decided to get a divorce because her mother was in love with another man and had sexual relations with him after not seeing him for almost 40 years.

In fact, the oldest son found out that his mother's life long love was his biological father. Now, why is this important? You see Mary Jane experienced challenges with men all of her life and would unconsciously sabotage relationships when they would become too close. Whenever she began to fall in love with a man and take the relationship to another level, she would make up a reason to end it. Not until she learned of her mother's love for another man and their affair did she begin to understand her own behavior and mindset. It was passed down to her from her mother.

I am of the mindset that what you believe is what you can become. You have to see it! But that means that you have to have the courage to rise above all of the noise of the people who says otherwise. Now, I am not naive to the fact that the force can be strong and overwhelming. That force can be so engrained in your mind that one can lose sight of their own dreams or even feel obligated to live within the expectations of others even when they are not in their own best interest. In addition, you may have to deal with jealous and envious family members and friends who see something special in you but don't want you to outshine them.

What's important is that you learn to Mind Your Mind by understanding who you are according to the Word of God. #ThinkAboutIt your unique purpose on this earth must outweigh others' expectations of you, especially if those expectations are not building you up.

Breaking negative generational challenges takes courage and a strong resolve. It requires transcending your mind above all that you know and what you've been told and what you have seen. It particularly requires being exposed to something different. Exposure is a critical aspect to change and success. If you never engage with others different than you in actions and words, then it is difficult to have a different perspective therefore different mindset.

Your strong resolve is not only for you but also for the generations to come. It is critical for you to share your story with the younger people in your life so that they can see the signs of negative generational patterns and manage them accordingly. Your courage to take on the challenge of establishing positive generational norms will pay off in ways that you will and will not get to see. Because you are a beneficiary of these generational challenges, doesn't mean that future generations have to be the benefactor of the same. Be determined that they will be a benefactor of courage to defy those challenges unapologetically.

That they will learn to be the boss of their own minds and diligently purge faulty thinking and behavior. Mastering Your MINDSET will be the key to your success during this life-long process. It is a life-long process because there will always be people and situations pulling at you so that you fail. Subsequently, there will also be people in your corner encouraging you. Hold on to those who are there to support you. It is a daily commitment. Sometimes you will feel the pull to conform to the unwanted generational behaviors and thinking, but once you recognize it you can manage and avoid going down those same roads. For many of us, our learned way of being is to try to make others ("they") happy by sacrificing our own happiness. But do not be mistaken, "they" are not interested in reciprocating the same. Break the cycle by walking the path you know to be right so future generations can inherit a new and more positive mindset.

#ThinkAboutIt: What generational challenges did you have to overcome? What generational challenges do you continue to face?

_____
_____
_____
_____
_____
_____
_____
_____
_____
_____
_____
_____
_____
_____
_____
_____
_____
_____
_____
_____
_____
_____

(extra notes pages at the back of the book)

Principle 3:

Mind Your MIND!
Quality Thoughts Are Everything—Guard Accordingly!

#ThinkAboutIt. The quality of your thoughts forms the quality of your life so it is imperative that you guard them accordingly. According to research on the mind, our minds are busy, busy, busy. Why so busy? Our minds generate thousands upon thousands of thoughts daily, some positive, some negative, and some unavoidable.

Regardless of the type of thought you have, each one produces a specific kind of energy. Quality thoughts are rooted in our ability to focus on positivity. So why do people spend so much time thinking negatively? Because negative thoughts are closely connected to our feelings of fear, guilt, and anger. These feelings are very strong and can control our outward behavior. In the book, *As a Man Thinketh*, written by James Allan (1903), he explains that each of us holds the key to every situation or thought and that paying attention to what we think about can transform us and the world around us.

Persistent negative thoughts can be overwhelming and cause anxiety and depression amongst other inappropriate feelings and behaviors. Everyone experiences negative thoughts from time-to-time and it is important to mind your mind so that those thoughts don't become recurring thoughts. This state of mind can lead to emotional imbalance which contributes to poor coping skills. #ThinkAboutIt. If you are constantly dealing with persistent negative thoughts you should seek out counseling to get to the root of it and to develop strategies to reduce or eliminate those thoughts. You can also read scripture that addresses the mind (Philippians 2:5 & Isaiah 26:3), read and recite positive affirmations or listen to upbeat music with a positive message. These strategies are necessary to get into the habit of thinking positively.

Are some thoughts unavoidable? Yes, whether they are positive or negative. They are natural thoughts we have when confronted with various types of experiences. They are triggered by reality or perception. Unavoidable thoughts can be connected to a smell, a sound, a taste, a voice, a touch, a color, an image. You get the point. Any one of those experiences will make you think about a person, place, or thing that either brought positivity or negativity to your life. Whatever the emotional experience, it doesn't tend to linger and is not recurring. It's a one time occurrence that triggers a certain memory.

Now positive thoughts are what you want to master. There is power in positivity:

- The power to be optimistic despite your circumstances
- The power to believe there is greater ahead
- The power to genuinely celebrate others
- The power to be self-reflective
- The power to calculate risks.

For some reason, some us are wired to go directly to negative thinking when faced with situations, but that state of mind does very little to help us to transform our thinking. Positive thinking helps to navigate the world with optimism.

You know there are some people who see the glass as half full instead of half empty. Half full means there is always room to grow. Half empty signifies that nothing else can be added. Positive thinking also helps to regulate your emotions, meaning that you remain centered even during the most difficult experiences. This mode of operation allows you to see beyond circumstances and arrive at place of hope and experience little worry. You tend to understand that all will be well no matter what. Positive thoughts should align with our actions and words. If not, train your mind to think positively and watch how your actions and words begin to reflect your thinking.

Mastering Your Positive State of Mind is also rooted in your spiritual belief system. It is contradictory to believe that there is a God who has all power and still move through the world with a negative state of mind. If this is you, examine why that is. Perhaps it has more to do with trying to control all aspects of your life instead of allowing God to guide your steps. Let's be clear, because you have a positive state of mind most of the time doesn't mean that you will not have negative thoughts. The difference is that you don't allow negative thinking to throw you off balance. Instead, you grab that thought before it gets deep into your brain and deal with it accordingly rather than continuously replaying those thoughts.

#ThinkAboutIt: What type of thinking is your typical modus operandi? Why?

_____

_____

_____

_____

_____

_____

_____

_____

_____

_____

_____

_____

_____

_____

_____

_____

_____

_____

_____

_____

_____

_____

_____

_____

_____

_____

_____

_____

_____

_____

(extra notes pages at the back of the book)

Principle 4:

Mind Your MIND!
"No More" Thinking

Free your mind and the rest will follow. Harness it's power. At some point in life, we all have to transition into 'No More" Thinking as a way of life or for a particular situation. This typically occurs for most people when they have just had enough. The goal here is to establish this mindset before you've had enough. Since most of us don't fall into this category, our "No More" Thinking often starts somewhere like: no more un-forgiveness, no more allowing people to use us, no more jealousy, no more not loving myself, no more depression, no more lying, no more putting everyone before me, no more living an unhealthy lifestyle, no more negative self-talk, no more comparing myself to others, no more allowing folks to take advantage of my kindness; no more believing what others have to say negatively about me, no more shame, no more guilt, no more being denied promotions, no more feeling unworthy of abundance, no more... no more...No More!

Transcending your thinking to "No More" will require courage and resolve. The courage to be unapologetically different with those close to you and the resolve to be who you are and to not go back when the pressure intensifies. Oh yes, it will definitely intensify because most people are not comfortable with change in others or themselves. They will think that you are being brand new and different. Your response should be that "I sure am, and love it!"

It is not ideal to just blurt out your "No More" Thinking to those around you. It's a process. It requires a well thought out conversation. How do you have such a conversation? Since the goal is to have the person hear what you are saying it may help to begin the conversation with 'I apologize for not sharing this with you sooner. I really need to share with you where I am in life." Yes, I said apologize. You see, we often allow people to do things to us or say things to us that we don't like and never address it until we have had enough. That person is then confused and wondering where the conversation is coming from. Their confusion can come across as defensive. That is the power of the apology, it sets the stage for the person to get into an active listening posture. Although you may feel like you don't need to apologize, this technique is very effective for engaging in courageous conversations. Try it but first write out what you want to say then read it back to yourself (out loud!) for tone and delivery. Use very few words—be succinct, clear, and concise.

Everybody, and I mean everybody has a story! Do not get comfortable with who "they" say you are, what "they" say you can and cannot do, what "they" say you must wear, and/or what "they" tell you to think or say. More often than not, "they" are constantly telling you that you are this or you not that, please understand their possible motives. There could be numerous underlying reasons that have absolutely nothing to do with you. You are just the target for them to release their mess on. You have to determine if you are the participatory target or the blind, unaware target.

If you are consistently the aim, you must ask yourself, what bullseye have I placed on myself? If the answer is that "they" achieve the intended effect, then you need to remove the bullseye in order for them to aim somewhere else. The good news here is that you have the choice to no longer be the target once you realize what's happening.

Now, if you are a blind or unaware target, you will have a lot of work to do to move from this space. This is a permission granted mindset but there hasn't been a conversation about it. Instead it's just the rules of the road "they" have established. It sometimes takes another person to point it out to you but please understand that this is where mastering your state of mind is going to be key. As you fight to transition to 'No More" Thinking in this area of your life, "they" will continue to aim those darts at you so that their intentions manifest. "They" will be confused about your change but you must have the mindset of what God says vs. what "they say." Who will you believe? Your modis operandi of a "No More" Thinking state of mind should be that you are a star and you will no longer sit on the bench for permission to transform your mind.

#ThinkAboutIt: What are your "No More" Thinking areas? How did you get there?

_____

_____

_____

_____

_____

_____

_____

_____

_____

_____

(extra notes pages at the back of the book)

Principle 5:

Mind Your MIND!
Linking Your Mindset to Your Purpose

Mastering Your State of Mind is easier to do when it is linked to your life purpose. What can be difficult to identify is your purpose especially when you are not pursuing it daily. If you have not identified your purpose yet, pose the following question to God. What were you created to do on this earth during this particular time? The key is to wait and listen for His response. While waiting, think about your daily interactions with others, the places you have traveled that you never thought you could go, those thoughts that seem to come out of no where and that you find yourself saying that can't be for me. God is perhaps trying to present you with your purpose. Find the link! It is the most liberating thing you can do for yourself. Train your mind to think in purpose.

Sadly, too many people state that they don't know their purpose. Wow, they are truly missing out on an opportunity to live life as they were created to do so. Will that be you? I urge you to not leave this earth never knowing your purpose. What do I mean? Think about it this way. For example, a lot of women hope to have children and/or to get married. So what if neither of these things happen? Then what? This a great example of how if this is what you believe your only purpose is when your thinking is limited. This is the reality for many women so there has to be more to this whole purpose thing. God does not make any mistakes. He is intentional! What are His intentions for you?

If this is where your thinking about purpose stops, then you are missing out on God's bigger purpose for your life. I've learned to link my thinking to my purpose while understanding that I was created to live here on earth at this particular time so that I can be of service to others, especially to women in the areas of self-confidence, self-worth, having a positive mind-set, loving themselves, and learning to be bold in the Holy Spirit. It's just that simple to me. So everyday, everything I think and everything I want do and say is linked back to my purpose. It is very clear to me that we are here to help take care of or support each other in some way. Now what that looks like is unique for each of us. What's your part in being of service to others according to your purpose? If you constantly link your thinking to what your purpose is or what you think it is, then and only then will you stay focused and your actions and your words will line up accordingly.

There is a cause and effect between your mindset and purpose. In other words, one is the result of the other. Make the connection with your thinking and actions. Once you have identified your purpose, you will begin to cause an effect in the world. This will be done intentionally and with strategy.

#ThinkAboutIt: Is your thinking linked to your purpose? How do you know?

_____
_____
_____
_____
_____
_____
_____
_____
_____
_____
_____
_____
_____
_____
_____
_____
_____
_____
_____
_____
_____
_____
_____
_____
_____
_____
_____
_____
_____

(extra notes pages at the back of the book)

Principle 6:

Mind your MIND!
Release Unwanted Captive Thoughts

All too often, many of us carry pointless and unprofitable thoughts. These thoughts are not very useful; in other words they are pointless. They can hinder our productivity. More importantly they can rob us of living life to its fullest and of our own unique purpose. You know some of these thoughts!

- I'm not good enough.
- I can't write that book.
- I will never be able to do that.
- My parents were a failure and so am I.
- My parents were perfect; therefore, I will never be able to live up to their expectations.
- My friends have more than I do so that makes them better than me.
- We were poor growing up so that makes us lower than everyone else.
- I am not as pretty or handsome as he/she so I am not going to shine my light.
- She/he is smarter than me.

And the list can go on and on and on and on......

Some of us have thought one or two of these thoughts at one point but we were able to let them go. They were just a passing thought.

In contrast, some of us have held on to these thoughts to the point that they have controlled how we move around the world. Not with confidence or pride. I'm here to tell you that you have to release those captive thoughts if you want to live life in purpose. This is where you solidify your power because those thoughts no longer control you and your every move. You will no longer be confined to your self-inflicted thoughts or what people have said about your thoughts.

Set yourself free from confined valueless thoughts. If your thoughts are not value added, then release them and replace them with productive value added captive thoughts.

Once you have replaced those thoughts, it is going to be important that you consistently replay them in your mind and apply them to your daily actions. Get into the habit of thinking positive self-fulfilling prophesies which are expectations about yourself that may effect your behavior in a manner that causes those expectations to be fulfilled. So why not think positively about yourself and imagine all of the dreams and goals you have envisioned coming true by seeing yourself in them? Seeing yourself in your mind first is the key to releasing those captive unmated thoughts.

#ThinkAboutIt: What unwanted captive thoughts do you need to release? What wanted captive thoughts will you replace them with?

_____

_____

_____

_____

_____

_____

_____

_____

_____

_____

_____

_____

_____

_____

_____

_____

_____

_____

_____

_____

_____

_____

_____

(extra notes pages at the back of the book)

Principle 7:

Mind Your State of MIND!
It's Transformative

The first six principles, when put into action on a daily basis, can be life changing. When you convert your thinking to shifting your mindset so that your view will change, recognize and minimize generational thinking challenges, engage in quality thoughts because they are everything—guarded accordingly, get into the habit of "No More" Thinking, linking your mindset to your purpose, and release those unwanted captive thoughts will lead to dramatic changes in your character, nature, and appearance. That's real and life-lasting transformation!

Engaging in the transformational process of learning how to shift your mindset will bring about pressures for you to remain the same. You have to remain steadfast and have vision. It cannot work if you downplay or undervalue the significance of this intentional shift in your state of mind. This encounter with yourself will open up a whole new world to you.

After this experience, you will never be the same. The personal and spiritual journey of life will continually renew itself in functional and transformative ways. You must first love God and then love yourself to sustain it. The sky is not the limit to what you can think because you can see the sky—what's beyond is where the transformation happens. Reforming and changing your state of mind can only come as a result of how you Mind Your MIND!

#ThinkAboutIt: Which of the six principles will you focus on immediately to begin Mastering Your State of Mind? Why? How will you take the next days to transform your mind and be purposeful with your thoughts? How will you put these principles into action?

_____

_____

_____

_____

_____

_____

_____

(extra notes pages at the back of the book)

Significance of Seven (7)

According to my research, the number seven (7) is the basis of God's word. It is the number of absoluteness physicality and spirituality. It is connected to God's creation of all things. There are also seven days in the week and God's Sabbath is on the seventh day. Jesus performed seven miracles on God's Holy Sabbath Day.

"And on the seventh day God finished his work that he had done, and he rested on the seventh day from all of his work that he had done." (Genesis 2:2; biblestudy.org)

From the numerology perspective, it also represents perfection, rest, security, and safety. It represents the thinker, the seeker, the teacher of truth. The mind of the 7 goes places other numbers rarely attain and are rational, flexible and hungry for knowledge. His/Her imagination is vast and powerful, which helps to guide him into the spiritual stratosphere few people ever reach where he/she puts much faith in the power of the mind. (numerology.com).

If you believe the biblical meaning of the number seven and can understand the numerology perspective of the number seven, then why not use these seven principles to Master Your State of Mind! Since the number 7 is for completeness, then that means you need to put an end to your faulty thinking and move into the number 8 phase of thinking which means new beginnings. You can then rest in knowing that you have established an effective process to Mind Your MIND.

As Luke 14:28 states, "Suppose one of you wants to build a tower. Won't you first sit down and estimate the cost to see if you have enough money to complete it"? #ThinkAboutIt – if you are hesitant about engaging in the daily process of Mastering Your Mindset, count the cost! I urge you to sit down and estimate the cost of not doing so and then estimate the profit of doing so. What is it costing you?

Review

The reality of life is that all of us struggle with our thoughts and the reality of our minds from time to time. Mind your MIND! reminds us to slow down and to take a purposeful approach towards our mindset as we move through our day. It is a reminder we could all use and a skill we could all be better at. This book will change your perspective and offer your mind a foundation of peace for years to come!

~ Carrie Woods
Corporate Leadership Development Specialist

Made in the USA
Lexington, KY
15 March 2018